Tiny Thoughtful Tidbits:

Small Sayings That Shape

Contents

* * *

Introduction

When thinking about your life, you have to consider the people who have helped shape you into the person you have become. From the time one is an infant all the way to adulthood, there have been people present. These individuals may have been parents, uncles, aunts, brothers, sisters, college professors, co-workers, pastors, or even yourself!

Yes, even you can come up with words of encouragement to inspire and dictate direction for your life. Many times in my own life, personal support has guided me through the toughest times. During challenging experiences the character of a person is developed. If there is no pressure, there can be no product.

Gold has to go through fire in order to make it to the market place. Wheat has to be sifted in order to be made into bread. Even an orange has to be crushed and pressed to make orange juice. Our lives are no different! Many times, we avoid the pressing, crushing and the difficult situations in order to make an "easier" path for our lives. The avoidance of the crushing, the pressing and difficult situations make us comfortable and not willing to explore new things, new ideas and new concepts. I have learned that the discovery of new explorations, the pressing, crushing, and trying situations can enrich our lives and make us better people.

Some of these situations may have been tiny in scope. As an adjective defined, tiny means very small and minute. At the time, the circumstance you encountered appeared huge because you were in the core of it. Once the time of testing was complete, and when you moved on from the matter, the situation, in retrospect, was tiny indeed. However, more and more of our character was formed, due to the tiny situations, that were instrumental in our lives.

The word thoughtful deals with something which requires some concern. Showing consideration for others or being considerate are examples of someone who is thoughtful. There have been many times where people have shown concern or care just by the words they have said. As these words had impact on my life when initially spoken, I realized very quickly these words were well thought out and were birthed out of a concern for my overall well being and future. Thoughtful and thought-felt words often have the most significant impact on lives. Concern and consideration could propel one toward the center of their called purpose.

Tidbits are a choice or pleasing bit of anything. Many of the things which have been said to me over the years have been bits of advice here and there which have added up to make a significant impact in my life. These tidbits can be gained through many, many ways. When putting something together, all the parts of the assembled product have a meaning, no matter how small they are. When putting things together, many times the smallest part is often the most significant part and the part which completes the product you are trying to put together. The same thing rings true with small, tidbit words.

Some words are powerful and are responsible for shaping our lives. For some people, these words become the difference between success and failure, starting and finishing, life and death. Words are spoken on a daily basis and oftentimes their strength is not realized in the changing of atmospheres. Many times, atmospheres can change as a result of what's spoken.

My father and mother greatly influenced my life with encouraging words and constant reminders of the twists and turns of life. This gave me the idea for this book. Words shape, form, create, and give direction to us. Many ideas which mold us are small in nature, but their effect can impact our lives as they did mine, even in my marriage, on my job and in other areas of my life.

The sections in this book include: personal life, employment, parental wisdom, faith, leadership, and a special section entitled "Up Together." In short, this is a book of thought provoking and motivational quotes to help move you to the place you were intended to be. If one quote changes the focus and direction of one life, then my mission has been accomplished!

Personal Life Quotes

In our lives there are quotes we can apply to our personal lives. Whether we are police officers, corporate executives, school teachers, garbage men, warehouse workers, or currently unemployed. Personally speaking, I have many quotes and words which have helped me.

Some of these words have come from other individuals, others have come in times where I've have had to encourage myself (These times have been many!) At any rate, our personal development is critical to our overall success in life and in whatever path we decide to take in life.

"If you look good, you feel good. When you feel good, you do good. When you do good, you are good."

-Cavell Samuels

Self image and perception is important in how we view ourselves. If you have a less than favorable view of yourself, you will not think of yourself in a high regard. However, if you view yourself in a favorable regard, you will view yourself in a different light.

Once this different view is realized, you will be able to say the following: "If you look good, you feel good. When you feel good, you do good. When you do good, you are good." How you feel often determines your overall effectiveness in what you do. In order to be effective, you must feel that you are an effective person.

"You have to do what you need to do to get done what needs to get done."

-Cavell Samuels

In my current profession, sometimes I find myself in stressful and possibly life-threatening situations, and when these conditions arise, action must take place quickly as inaction could be detrimental. This is where training becomes relevant.

By profession, I am a trained responder. I reply to the actions of others. In responding, the scenarios I may be faced with may not come as experienced in training. This is when untrained means or instinct kicks in to handle the situation. This is doing what you have to do to get done what needs to get done.

In our lives, there are things we know we need to handle. In the handling of these things, we are doing what we have to do in order to get done what needs to get done. Getting things done takes personal responsibility on our end. Getting things done can mean any and everything.

No matter what needs to be accomplished, no matter what needs to take place, there has to be some action, some effort, and some energy given to accomplish what needs to be done. The understanding and application of personal responsibility is key in the understanding of the aforementioned quote.

"Love folks and you will live long!"

-Elder Jettie Cornett, Pastor, Greater Grace Temple COGIC

I recently heard this stated by the pastor of my home church during a recent teaching. In this day and time, it is critical that we love others. It is through this demonstration of love and concern for our fellow man which makes our world a better place to live in, and in turn, make our lives more fruitful and longer, as stated in the mentioned quote.

Remember, love folks, and you will live long!

"You can't expect different results if you are not doing differently."

-Cavell Samuels

I've heard many people say they want to do things differently. Yet, when these same people get done talking, it seems like they are doing the same thing. I know this is true when I see them in the same position time and time again.

Different steps equal different results. I did not realize I had the time to write this book until I started to wake up earlier in the day and watch less television. The sleep time and the television time I had before is now being utilized to write this book you are reading!

If I continued to watch television and sleep in, you would not be reading these pages now. I started doing different, and now I'm seeing different as a result of this change of habit.

"You have to alter a particular thing in order to have control."

-Cavell Samuels

Alterations are adjustments made to fit the particular person or entity needing these alterations. In making these alterations, the person is saying the particular thing being altered does not fit their standards. In other words, they are controlling the fit of the item on their bodies. In order for us to have control in certain areas of our lives (health, finances, and the like) we may need to alter what we are doing.

Once we make the proper alterations, we will have more control over the particular area we are trying to alter. With more control, comes more freedom. Alterations at times have to be made in order for us to better control the areas of our lives which need controlling!

"Turn your excuses into energy to head in the right direction."

-Cavell Samuels

It's so easy to make excuses as to why something was not completed. I was tired, I did not know, I was going to do it, but….All of these are examples of excuses. I have taken some of the excuses I had, and turned them into energy to eliminate those same excuses. I use to make the excuses of my working 2nd Shift, and getting off at 10:30 at night as justification for sleeping in. Instead of using these reasons as an excuse, I now wake up NO LATER THAN 7:30AM each day. Many days, I am up a lot earlier.

I used to make the excuse of not having the time to pray. Now I have taken that excuse and turned this into having the energy to pray when I wake up first thing in the morning! Utilize your excuses and turn them into energy you need to execute your plans. Believe me, it works!

"You can't rob Peter to pay Paul, and then rob Saul to pay them all!"

-Cavell Samuels

If one has issues in one hand, and issues in the other hand, one cannot go to another set of issues to resolve the issues found in the other two hands. The saying "Two wrongs don't make a right" is the perfect summary of this quote. Violence cannot eliminate violence, only peace can eliminate violence. Broke can't resolve broke…..but if rich enters the equation, broke times will go away.

Peter, Paul and Saul all have problems…..problems do not solve problems, only solutions can solve problems!

"Don't forsake the lessons learned by taking small steps. Little by little, you will make it."

-Cavell Samuels

My daughter and I were at home one day, and I took her by the hand. I began to say to her little by little, step by step, little by little step by step. She repeated after me, and just by taking small steps, we found ourselves in the kitchen of our home.

The main lesson I drew from this experience was to take the first step! If we didn't take the first step, we wouldn't make it to the kitchen. Secondly, when taking the first step, we had to place one of our feet in front of the other.

Progression comes in steps, but when you don't take the first step, progression will not take place. Little by little, step by step, you will make it!

"Accountability is the new profane word."

-*Cavell Samuels*

Accountability is very difficult to grasp and embrace, especially when being held accountable by someone else. But it's through accountability we are moved and motivated to change. This is a hard truth, but many are not willing to be held accountable in these days and times.

When accountability comes, it seems like an attack to many individuals today. However, we must begin to embrace accountability and not view accountability as being profane.

Employment

Everyone, regardless of their age will eventually have to work in order to make a reasonable and decent living for themselves or their families. Employment, by definition, means the condition of having paid work, or the action of providing paid work to someone.

Employment is essential in this day and time, and lessons learned through employment can remain with you for years to come. The next pages involve quotes which I have learned through my various employment experiences.

"If you play fast break, I play half court. If you play half court, I play fast break."

-Cavell Samuels

There are times when things are going so fast! When things are moving at a quick pace, you must slow down! At my job, I often tell this to the people I oversee on a regular basis. I'll be the one dictating the tempo I work, and not the people I oversee. In life, we many times are the ones that dictate what happens to us, and can determine the outcomes in many situations we are faced with.

Tempo control is key in music, sport, and is also key in our everyday lives. When things are fast-paced and borderline chaotic, take the time to slow things down. However, when things seem to be moving at a slow pace, feel free to pick up the tempo. Either way, a healthy balance of tempo control will take you a long way.

"When training or teaching, it's important to always demonstrate the "why" in what you are teaching or training."

-Cavell Samuels

I often refer to myself as a Field Education Officer at my job. My actual job title is Field Training Officer. Teaching reveals the "why" to the students who are being taught. Once someone knows why they are doing things, many things will begin to make sense to them. Training says "yes or no," education shows why. Once the "why" is known, the knowledge obtained is applied and utilized in a wise manner.

Knowing why you do a particular thing opens up doors. Knowing why puts a purpose to your plan.

Knowing why can make a difference in whatever you are doing! Demonstrate the "why" so you know why!

"If one is mediocre long enough they will think mediocrity is normal. Be sure to practice excellence. Excellence will become normal."

-Cavell Samuels

Mediocrity will lure you into stagnation, routine, and complacency. However, when you practice excellence, this excellence will push you to strive to be the best you can be. When excellence is consistent, we will begin to display excellence in our lives.

If we practice being excellent in our lives, we will see the results. The only way to be excellent is to acknowledge the Lord Jesus Christ in what we do, because He is the standard of excellence!

"Many times, employment is a means to an end, a step toward the place where one is intended to be."

-Cavell Samuels

This was revealed to me while at work one day. Many choose to stay and work in a profession they do not like, making it a career. A career is something you enjoy to do; a job is something you have to do. I am of the persuasion that one should enjoy what they do.

When what you have to do merges with what you enjoy doing, this is what I call a full life and career. When moving toward what you enjoy (career) you must keep in mind that employment provides the necessary steps to get to your intended destination.

Remember to grow where you are, learn and apply the lessons learned in the current place you are in. Remember, it's just a means to an end!

"Your job is what you do, not who you are!"

-Cavell Samuels

In life you will find or encounter many in society who feel their job or occupation defines who they are. We see this, especially with men in our society. As a man, I have observed many men define who they are by what they do.

In this context, who I am outweighs what I do. There are many hats one may wear, but we must keep in mind that the hats we wear are to be left at the various places we consider to be employment. Simply put, keep your work at work! Remember, what you do is not who you are!

Parental Wisdom

Parents have given many of us timeless and relevant advice, words of warning, and words of guidance. My parents Freddie and Mary Samuels have said many, many things which have shaped my life.

I hope the following words help you in your life in one way or the other. Please take heed, and enjoy!

"Don't struggle if you don't have to!"

-Freddie Samuels

These words literally changed my life! I was in a place in life when I really needed to hear this. It was before I married my wife. My father and I had a talk in the den of his home about having insurance and having meaningful employment before taking care of a family.

My father worked two or more jobs throughout my growing up; working to provide for my mother and me, so these words rang true to me. There is strength in the struggle I know, but just make sure your struggle is not a self-inflicted struggle. These words from my father rang true then, and they ring true now!

Part of the struggle is gaining strength. We understand the unnecessary struggle is not wise and can be detrimental to us. Unnecessary struggle does not yield fruitful results. Don't struggle, if you don't have to!

"The Lord does things in His timing."

-Mary Samuels

It was 2010, and my wife and I were in the process of attempting to conceive our daughter. We had tried for about three years to that point, and I had shared this with my mother. After I got done talking, my mother stated the aforementioned quote. I did not get it at the time, but I really get it now.

We oftentimes try to figure out the timing of the Lord, but this will cause us to fail every time. This is why it is essential for us to trust in the Lord. At the time we did not understand what the Lord was doing, but in 2011, the Lord saw fit to bless us with our beautiful daughter - in His time!

His time can be confusing. His time can be frustrating. His timing can honestly seem terrible, but we must truly understand that the Lord does things in His time!

"You can do anything you put your mind to."

-Freddie Samuels

My father is the most instrumental person in my life. All while growing up; my father would continually tell me that I could do anything I put my mind to.

I know many of you, as you read this are probably thinking I had a "perfect" childhood and my father was the perfect father. This is not correct, but I realize more and more everyday that my father is the perfect father for me. Through his trials, tribulations, and situations he endured in his life, his wisdom and instruction were critical in my upbringing.

Through these words of affirmation and approval, I have begun to apply this to my life and have told my daughter the same thing. The power of the mind is a vital tool we can utilize to move forward in our respective life assignments. As a man thinks, so is he! Therefore, once we place our minds on a particular task or tasks, we more than likely will set out and complete these task or tasks.

"You can't do everything at once. Take your time and get done what you can get done."

-Freddie Samuels

My father provided this lesson during a time where I was working 16 hour days. During this time, my grass had grown pretty high, and my yard did not look up to standard, according to me. It was then my father said you can't do everything at once. You are working and doing other things, so select a time to take care of what you can, and save the rest for another time.

This tidbit of information taught me a little bit of something is a better than a whole lot of nothing. I have learned through this advice that life is a marathon and not a sprint. There are times you will get many things done, but will neglect your family in turn. I have taken this principle and utilized this time and time again, and it has paid big dividends for me.

Faith

Faith, in short is the ability to step out and do things when all the "P's and Q's" do not add up. It's functioning when things seem to be non-functional. Faith, in short, believes in something which cannot be seen or felt in a tangible way.

Faith is very essential in the lives of people, and is essential to success.

"The Lord needs a vessel to work through. That vessel is you. The Lord works through His people."

-Elder Jettie Cornett, Pastor, Greater Grace Temple COGIC.

I heard this one Sunday morning while at my current home church. This profound statement eliminates all laziness and excuses. Many times, we want the Lord to do something for us, but many times we are not willing to sacrifice the effort, time or energy to be used of the Lord for His work.

We must be a willing vessel in order for His power and glory to be manifested on and in this earth. If we are unwilling, we cannot expect for the work to be done. Romans 12:1 puts it like this: "I beseech you therefore, brethren, by the mercies of God, that ye present your bodies a living sacrifice, holy, acceptable unto God which is your reasonable service."

If you are a disciple of Jesus Christ, you have a requirement to be used for effective service. Be a willing vessel, then you can be used!

"Unity begins with the letter "U" and each one of us!"

-Cavell Samuels

Psalm 133:1 reads "Behold, how good and pleasant it is for brethren to dwell together in unity." Unity ultimately begins with the individual, meaning it begins with you! As you are reading, and desire to have unity in your city, town and community, keep in mind you must be the change you want to see.

Unity is also a major part of faith as well. We have to believe in others and the power of working together if we are going to experience effective change.

"Mentalities have to change, and the change has to begin mentally, with us. If we embrace this change, we will be better servants to and for our people."

-Cavell Samuels

A change of anything has to begin with the person or agent who needs to be changed! No transformation will take place unless the person to be transformed acknowledges this fact. Change must begin with the individual.

The mind is where many of our setbacks, hesitations, and defeats take place, so when the mind is hindered, no effective change can take place. Once the shift in mindset and change of mindset takes place, one will begin to experience true change.

"Transformation without renewing equals destruction. Renewal is a critical element in overall change."

-Cavell Samuels

Romans 12:2-"And be not conformed to this world: but be ye transformed by the renewing of your mind, that ye may prove what is that good, and acceptable, and perfect will of God." In this scripture you see the essence of being renewed. It is in renewing true transformation takes place! In order for effective change to take place, renewal is a must!

When we are transformed according to our standards, we will fail every time, and eventually be destroyed. We must line up our standard of transformation with the Word of the Lord!

"A changed purpose will bring about a new perspective with forward progress!"

-Cavell Samuels

The word purpose gets thrown around on a regular basis. What is my purpose, what am I here for? Our purpose is outlined in the Word of the Lord.

When man was created in Genesis, he gave man the assignment to till the ground and to keep it. We, as men were designed to work, to protect and provide for our wives and children! This is our purpose, to be Godly fathers, Godly protectors, and Godly providers of natural as well as spiritual things.

Once we have this perspective, we will have new forward progress!

"The main trick of the enemy is to draw believers away from the reading, studying and application of the word of the Lord."

-Cavell Samuels

Many times when I am blessed to share in teaching, I open up with the aforementioned statement. When you are drawn away from the word of the Lord, you are setting yourself up to be deceived and tricked.

Whenever you want to know the truth of anything, as it relates to your walk as a believer, line it up with the Word. When it lines up with the Word, you will be drawn to the Lord, instead of drawn away from the Lord.

"Prayer brings about action. Effective prayer is preparation to propel one into action."

-Cavell Samuels

What is prayer? We must understand that it is communication with Jesus Christ. In Luke 18:1, in part it states that men ought to always pray, and not faint. In this, it is critical that we continually communicate with the Lord in prayer.

Once prayer has taken place, there is to be a corresponding action which accompanies prayer.

"Recalling eliminates routine and moves us toward deeper relationship."

-Cavell Samuels

Lamentations 3:21-23 reads, "This I recall to my mind, therefore have I hope. It is of the Lord's mercies we are not consumed, because his compassions fail not. They are new every morning: great is thy faithfulness."

It is in these scriptures that Jeremiah recalls the good times while going through his dark times. This is the essence of our relationship with the Lord Jesus Christ. Each day we are given, we need to recall who provides all of our blessings!

"Fear is the biggest obstacle to any progress."

-Cavell Samuels

The Word of the Lord in 2 Timothy 1:7 declares: "God has not given us the spirit of fear, but of power, love and a sound mind!" Fear has the ability to handicap, hinder, and halt any forward progress one may make.

When moving forward, fear is not an option! There is too much for one to do to operate in fear. Move from fear and move toward making faith moves in your life! Faith requires a move from fear and a move toward making steps which will improve one's situation.

"When we entertain instead of edify, we damage instead of deepen."

-Cavell Samuels

Entertainment, by definition means to detain for something to enter in. In a worship context, when our main focus is to please and move people instead of pleasing the Lord, we are damaging the ones who are attending our worship services.

The Bible teaches in Psalm 47:6 to "Sing praises to God, sing praises: sing praises unto our King, sing praises." All we do as believers is unto the Lord, and not unto men. When we make our focus men, we will be engaging in the pride of life as defined in 1 John the second chapter.

When reading further in that chapter, it is written that he who does the will of the Lord abides forever (1 John 2:17). We are mandated to edify the body in Ephesians 4. It is through the edification of the body of Christ that roots are deepened. When we edify, we deepen. When we entertain, we damage.

Leadership

One will have to deal with leadership in one capacity or another. One will either be the top leader, lead from the middle or report to someone who leads. There are components and keys which are important in leadership.

I am no leadership expert, but I've had opportunities to influence and have significant input on decisions which were made on my job and in work outside of my main source of income.

Understanding leadership is key in making a move forward in any area of life.

"Leadership externally cannot take place without internal leadership."

-Cavell Samuels

If you are going to be an effective leader, you have to be led! The internal leading of the Lord Jesus Christ is key in your being an effective leader. With the Lord leading you internally, this influence and guidance will begin to show on the outside. You cannot lead without being led by the Holy Ghost!

When you are led by the Holy Ghost, this is the essence of true leadership!

Examples of this in scripture are found in Ephesians 4 and Matthew 5.

External leadership demands internal leadership! To simplify this, to lead effectively, you have to be Spirit led!

"True leadership and inconsistency do not mix. You cannot effectively lead being inconsistent."

-Cavell Samuels

Being inconsistent speaks to many different issues and concerns. Inconsistency in leadership is unacceptable. When you, as a leader are inconsistent, others on your team will be inconsistent. As a leader, one must make sure you are consistent in whatever you do.

Just like oil and water, leadership and inconsistency do not mix. If inconsistency in leadership is observed, it will be noticed by those being led. Remember, people being lead can often see when leadership is "Off." Being consistent is key in being an effective leader.

"If you can't stand conflict, you will conform!"

-Cavell Samuels

Conflict is a part of life. Conflict also breeds productivity and growth as well. I have learned the most about myself when I have been challenged. However, if you run from conflict, you will ultimately conform to your environment that you are in. It is through conflict that the greatest changes often take place.

If you don't have conflict, you will more than likely remain the same. But for change, conflict is necessary.

The type of conflict I'm talking about is not a violent type of conflict, but conflict which challenges what you stand for and what motivates you internally.

"Conflict births courage. If you are willing to be confronted, you are willing to be courageous."

-Cavell Samuels

Being confronted is a difficult thing to deal with. As a part of human nature, people try to avoid areas of conflict at all costs! But there are times in which conflict has to take place. It's through conflict that courage is birthed and character is shaped.

You would not know you are courageous if you were never confronted. These confrontations could be physical in nature. Conflict also takes place emotionally, psychologically and even spiritually. The willingness of someone being courageous often hangs on the amount of conflict. Most of the successful movements in this country were birthed in conflict.

From the Civil War to the Civil Rights Movement, the one element all of these movements have in common is a sense of conflict. However, it was through this conflict, the most courageous Americans were discovered.

"If you are scared to shoot, you are scared to succeed. Be willing to step up and take the shot! With every shot attempt, there is a chance for success."

-Cavell Samuels

I played basketball during my younger years. I was an ok basketball player. I would have been better if I were willing to take more shots! In taking a shot, there is apprehension, and there may be some fear in doing so, but the more you shoot, the more your probability increases in you making the shot!

In taking the shot, your chances to succeed also increase! You limit your chances when you don't take the shot! Take the shot! Your chances of success will rise when you do this. It may be difficult, but take the shot, you can make it!

Up Together

About two years ago, I was introduced to a young man by my mother by the name of Cortney Sargent who has a motto which states, "Let's make it better by going up together!" This is not only a catchy phrase, but is a way of life. Making others better around you makes everyone else better.

This young man was definitely sent by the Lord Jesus Christ to me, and I value his friendship greatly. The following pages are quotes which have been shared by Cortney Sargent on his radio broadcast, "Up Together with Cortney Sargent."

"One of the things that kills direction is procrastination. Lack of motivation breeds procrastination."

-Cortney Sargent

Procrastination is the act of putting off something. This could be work related, home related or even family related. When we put off, we will be less motivated to complete. This is why we must be motivated and complete all of what's required of us.

We have to get motivated so we won't procrastinate. It is in procrastination the lack of direction is birthed. If you don't want to head in a particular direction, procrastinate. If you procrastinate, you will stop all movement and be stuck in a rut.

"Thanksgiving unlocks the fullness of life to you. Being thankful is a mental perception. It will turn chaos into peace."

-Cortney Sargent

Being thankful is a mindset and a lifestyle. If we do not embrace thankfulness, we will find ourselves in an unthankful state. Once in this unthankful state, we will not be fulfilled but will be unfulfilled.

With everything that is going on in your life now, one must still remain thankful in all things that happen and take place. But once we remain thankful and grateful, we will begin to see our chaotic situations turn peaceful as a result of our thankfulness to the Lord.

Unlock the fullness of life, be thankful!

"In order to get to the next, you have to maximize the now!"

-Cortney Sargent

There is a song which says, "Right now, right now, let the Savior bless your soul right now! Don't you put off until tomorrow what you can do today, let the Savior bless your soul right now!" The power and relevance in the lyrics of that one song summarize the aforementioned quote.

Many times in life, we all have been guilty of saying this can wait, or that can wait. But in doing this, we must ask ourselves an important question, and that question is: Are we maximizing our now? Get to the next, maximize the now, right now!

"If you do not live to help somebody else, your life is not worth living!"

-Cortney Sargent

This one quote speaks volumes and is a testament of how I try to live my entire life. If you are living just to help yourself, you will be the only one who benefits. However, if we live to serve our fellow man, and live to help others tap into their unknown potential, our world would be a better place.

I firmly believe the reason I am living is to help others. This is what the Bible calls a servant. Serving involves one letting their personal feelings and ideologies go in order to enhance the lives of others. Again, if you do not live to help somebody else, your life is not worth living.

Special Acknowledgement and Dedication

Two very special people have made the writing of this book possible. These special people are Freddie and Mary Samuels, my parents. I have learned so much through their example over my 36 years of life, and I am thankful that I was given to such wonderful people. You are loved and are appreciated!

Acknowledgements

- To my Lord, Savior and King Jesus Christ. The exchange of my life for your life was made, and for that I am grateful. My prayer is that the will of the Lord Jesus Christ be done.

- To my beautiful wife, Shiraune. I affectionately call you "My Beautiful Queen." You have been a wonderful supporter of all I have stepped out and done. You are the one encouraging me and praying for me. I don't deserve such an excellent wife as you! I pray we will continue to grow in Christ and with one another. #TeamSamuels

- To my wonderful daughter, Kerrington. You motivate and inspire Daddy everyday! As I am writing this out, you are on my lap right now. I am thankful to the Lord that he blessed us with such a wonderful blessing!

- To my Pastor Jettie L. Cornett, Assistant Pastor Jerry Cornett, and the entire Greater Grace Temple Church of Racine, Wisconsin. During the 10 years I have been a part, I have grown in many different ways. I thank the Lord that he has entrusted me to serve such a wonderful body of believers in the Lord Jesus Christ!

- To Cortney Sargent and Family. Cortney, I started listening to your radio show in August of 2014. It was then I knew you were someone I had to reach out to. Through reaching out to you, I have learned so much, and have been taken from neutral, and placed into drive. My friend, keep doing what you are doing……this is only the beginning!

- To my editors, Tara Pringle Jefferson and Mrs. Pearl Terry. Thank you for taking the time out to edit this book. I thank you both for your critique and honest opinions.

- To Alphonzo Ashworth. I had the pleasure of meeting you for the first time in Chicago in 2015, and I have valued your insight, wisdom and stand for truth ever since. Thank you for your

words, insight, and honest way
you present things.

- To the late Leslie W. Jennings,
  Jr. While in the process of
  finalizing this book, Mr.
  Jennings passed away. I am
  thankful I had the chance to
  know you. Continue to rest in
  the Lord.

About the author

Cavell Samuels is a man of integrity, honesty and hard work, who has the passion and desire to see things done in the spirit of excellence. During his formative years, he was raised in the Greater Mount Eagle Baptist Church in Racine, Wisconsin. As a result of this upbringing in the church, a life-long seed of service in the house of the Lord was planted inside of him.

Cavell was accepted to Tennessee State University in Nashville, Tennessee, where he majored in Criminal Justice, and minored in Psychology, graduating with a Bachelor of Science degree in Criminal Justice in May of 2002.

During this time, he was surrounded by brilliant academic minds, which he gives credit to for shaping him, and laying much of the foundation for him in his formative years.

In addition to the previously mentioned, Cavell has also served his state civically through the Governor's Juvenile Justice Commission, appointed by former Wisconsin governor Jim Doyle, serving in the year of 2004.

In November of 2014, Cavell founded Kingdom First Consulting, LLC, whose main aim is to provide training, fellowship opportunities, and resources for those who are involved in areas of providing ministry assistance through administration in churches and ministries. In January of 2015, he received certification as a Church Administrator from the International Association of Certified Church Administrators.

Personally, Cavell is happily married his wife, Shiraune, and is the proud father of their daughter, Kerrington.

Cavell's main desire is that the will of the Lord be done in all areas of his life, and in the lives of others, according to St. Matthew 6:10: "Thy kingdom come. Thy will be done in earth, as it is in heaven."